DESPERATE
for
Change

Life with a Chronic Illness:
A story of grit and perseverance in the
pursuit of a life worth loving

John R. Porta Jr.

First paperback edition December 2020
 ISBN 9798573446554

Chapter 1

The Story

The exam room was cold, brightly lit, and echoing with muffled voices from down the hall. The young man sat impatiently waiting for the Physician's Assistant to return with his MRI results. Seconds felt like minutes, minutes felt like hours. He thought, I'm 31 years old, yeah the headaches were pretty bad, but the last few days my head felt fine. It must have been a nasty sinus infection.

As he grew more restless, he hopped out of his chair and began pacing the room, planning the remainder of his day. He believed everything was going to be fine, but the way the MRI technician inquired about the timing of his follow-up appointment made him a little uneasy. Nah, the headaches are gone... everything is fine, he reassured himself.

After what felt like an eternity, the door opened and he sat down like a student caught out of his seat during class. The PA walked in holding the MRI results. He looked anxious.

Uh oh, the patient thought. He could feel his heart rate increasing and rubbed his sweaty palms.

The PA started, "I am sorry, but the MRI images showed…"

Breathe, just breathe, the patient reminded himself silently.

"A tumor."

The PA continued speaking, but the man's mind was gone, racing away. He was thinking about his newborn daughter and his beautiful wife. He was just trying to keep his emotions in check.

His awareness returned in time to hear about the follow-up appointment with a neurosurgeon in Pittsburgh. At the check-out desk, his emotions started flooding in. *How? Why? Is this it?* He tried his hardest not to let the tears roll out and politely thanked the receptionist as she handed him an appointment card.

He got to his car, closed the door, and lost it. Emotions poured out, tears flowed, prayers begged for a miracle. Taking a deep breath felt impossible. He needed to talk with someone. His wife was at work and he didn't want to upset her in the middle of her work day. He needed to calm down first. He sat and wept.

How about my dad, he thought. *I need help. I don't know what to do.* He dialed the phone. His father's hesitant hello at the other end of the line sounded worried. Everyone had been worried about him, this he knew... but a *tumor* was just too real and scary to imagine. He attempted to say hello, but had no voice; no words came out of his mouth.

"Hello! What's wrong?" asked his worried father.

How can you talk if you can't breathe? You can't. He tried again. "I have a tumor..."

Silence.

The father is a supportive, stubborn man. He coached athletes for his entire adult life. Immediately, he went into planning mode. "Where are you?"

The younger man was starting to find his voice. "In my car, outside the doctor's office." His father told him to go to their house and see his mother before he started the 30-minute drive home.

As he drove, the man couldn't stop thinking of his wife and daughter. He had no clue what the future may hold but he decided he was going to do everything he needed to, for them. As he walked into his parents' house he was ready to investigate the MRI results, but he still wasn't quite prepared to see his mother. Apparently, the young man looked awful and that can cause some major anxiety for a mother.

"What's wrong? What happened?" she asked.

Here we go again, he thought. Can't breathe, tumor, tears.... Is this a thing now?

"I need your laptop." His determination re-emerged. Pulling out his MRI results, he began to research.

Macroadenoma? Um okay. Let's go, Google.

Pituitary Tumor? Okay so not in my brain, but attached and a little below it. That has to be better than *in* it.

Pituitary Gland? Like a master command center. Wait did that say...? Yup, it sure did. Usually non-cancerous. Wahoo! Now we are talking. What else?

Can cause panhypopituitarism. Um, wow. That is a long word.

Need lots of lab work. Oh yeah, I have a lab slip somewhere.

Video on surgery. Yup, shouldn't have watched that.

Surgeon can remove the tumor through the nose?!?! Ouch! What? How?

So, I might live. I can breathe a little, he thought. This is going to be hard but possible.

His phone rang... ignored. He needed to know more. The phone rang again. *Can I even talk yet?* he wondered. I can't scare my wife. It rang a third time. *Okay, you need to answer. You're scaring your wife,* he told himself. *Breathe, say hello.*

"How was the appointment?" she asked.

He started with everything he knew. "I have a tumor, most likely not cancerous. An appointment with a neurosurgeon is scheduled and I am going to be alright. We got this!"

The next nine months were the worst of his entire existence on this planet. Lab work, MRI to find out the tumor hasn't shrunk, new medicines, more lab work, side effects, different medicines, another MRI with the same results, even more lab work, and on and on. He tried so hard to be normal, but the combination of the side effects of his new medications and the symptoms of his new illness made it impossible. He was experiencing weight gain, hair loss, EXTREME fatigue, more weight gain, and an introduction to anxiety and depression. Throw that on top of being a new dad and just getting out of bed in the morning became a huge accomplishment.

During this time he learned what Pituitary Apoplexy meant, basically a tumor cut off the blood supply to his pituitary gland and caused it to infarct or die. That explained the terrible headaches he was experiencing before his diagnosis. *His pituitary gland was dead* with little hope of it regaining function.

He started to wonder if this was his life now. How could he exist like this? How could he survive with no motivation or energy to do anything? What kind of life could he expect when feeling anxious, or having uncontrollable sadness all the time with no relief?

My wife and daughter don't deserve this, he thought. *Will my wife leave me? Can this really be my life now?*

The man tried to go on vacation with his family to Myrtle Beach, so he could relax and attempt to feel normal. WRONG!!! The anxiety of the trip ruined every second and memories of that vacation scarred him for years.

One thing about 31 year old men is that they don't want to show weakness. He tried to fake it for his family, but a week together was too long to hide his troubles. After that vacation, his wife was no longer the only one who knew how truly sick he was and how badly he was struggling. The secret was out.

The man lived with anxiety attacks, tears, marathon naps, extreme sadness, and more naps. He wanted to hide, but there was nowhere to go. He couldn't shake the anxiety; the feeling that something was *terribly* wrong, but he didn't know what. The only thing that stopped the panic attacks was medication that left him feeling like he'd turned off his brain. It made him so tired he couldn't keep his eyes open.

The cycle needed to stop. It was time for surgery. No more tumor shrinking pills with awful side effects! ENOUGH! The neurosurgeon agreed and surgery was scheduled. Time for more anxiety, just waiting for a doctor to go inside your head and remove a tumor.

The drive to Pittsburgh with his wife was quiet. They were both nervous about the surgery and it was the first time they'd been away from their one year old daughter. He was ready, but scared. *What ifs* played non-stop in his head. *What if* they nick the carotid artery and I bleed out, or an optic nerve and I lose vision? What if the neurosurgeon sneezes while he's in my head removing the tumor? Will I have nose issues after a tumor is yanked out of it?

They were joined at the hotel by his parents, sister, and brother-in-law. Talk about a weird vibe, he thought. So awkward. They attempted a normal night, with pizza and a board game. His dad won.

"REALLY!" the young man exclaimed. "Yinz couldn't let me win?"

They made it an early night because it would be an early morning. Not much sleep was had that night in any of their rooms.

He thought he was ready for surgery but how could he be? He tried to convince himself that everything would be alright, but he had zero control. At the hospital, he went through the motions and did what he was told. Chest X-ray, strip down and put on a hospital gown. Kiss the wife, tell everyone you love them, and pray.

Two neurosurgeons, an ear, nose, throat doctor, nurses, an anesthesiologist, and a group of student doctors took his life into their hands for a few hours. Let that sink in. They were going to be in the middle of his head. How could he prepare for that? He couldn't, so he went through the motions. Hospital bed, count backwards: 10, 9, 8, 7, siiixxx......

Voices, crying, blood pressures, stupid intern doctors. Waking up was hard for him. "The tumor is gone," he hears someone say... or was it a dream? Oh good, I must be alive, he thought. Crying, why is there crying? He hears his father telling his sister to go to work the next day. He thinks he must look pretty crappy because she was apparently scared to leave. Vomiting blood, and vomiting again. Medicine for nausea, repeat MRI... nevermind, vomiting. Anesthesia sucks, he thought. Can't stay awake.....gooooodnight.

Silence, total stillness. His eyes opened slowly. Everything was blurry; his contacts were missing. His room was empty. It was the middle of the night. A nurse walked in with a smile on her face. "You did well", she said. "The tumor was removed and they believe they got it all!"

The surgery was a success. He exhaled and found his glasses. What a feeling of relief. He couldn't put his excitement and relief into words. He just smiled as his eyes focused on the picture sitting on his hospital bed tray: his tiny, redheaded daughter. And now the real story can begin....

Chapter 2

Reset Button

Anyone can relate to this story. Maybe it sounds like you, your neighbor, a relative, or a friend. It could be anyone. The point actually isn't the story. I am writing because of the opportunity the story presents: the opportunity to start over or reset. The young man in the story was defeated but surgery gave him hope and a fresh start.

The story is my story. I was the scared 31 year old, a new father who had everything to lose. I never considered what I might gain. Just to be clear - I am not a writer, I don't have a PhD or MD after my name, I am not a research scientist, and I didn't find some magical RESET button to push. I am simply an individual who has learned to succeed with a chronic illness and is writing to help someone else who may be struggling and needs encouragement to face their adversities. When I was newly diagnosed 10 years ago, I needed to know that everything was going to be okay. I needed to know that I wasn't alone. I needed to know that life would get better. I am writing this book for that individual who was in my shoes 10 years ago.

That is why I am sharing my story. I don't care how many books I sell. I have zero aspirations of being a best-selling author. I will probably never write another book, but I hope this book finds its way to someone, anyone who might be feeling alone in their struggles, and I hope I can help at that moment.

So as I sat in that hospital bed alone, I just stared at my daughter's picture. She was my strength. I needed to be my best for her. After surgery, I wasn't allowed to return to work for five weeks. It was time to get my life in order.

It is kind of crazy how life can come in and make you reevaluate everything you are doing. It doesn't have to be an illness, either. Maybe you have a newborn, lose a job, turn 40 years old... or maybe COVID-19 comes along and changes the world. Let me give you one more option - do it yourself! Set up a plan, and change your life. I am going to walk you through what works for me. Just FYI, I don't have all the answers. I stumble, I lose focus, I haven't studied the field for 40 years, but what I am proud to say is that I LOVE MY LIFE and I have a desire to help you achieve your goals.

I told you about my extreme fatigue and weight gain when I was really sick. Well, I have spent most of my life at about 175 to 185 lbs. I am 5'8" so I wasn't really skinny in the first place. When I went for surgery, I was 240 lbs. I still have a picture that my wife took of me, lying in the hospital bed after surgery, sleeping, of course. WOW, did I look awful! That picture is a constant reminder of the opportunity I have every day to improve upon myself and to never return or forget where I've been. So my first step was to get in shape.

How did a college athlete balloon to 240 lbs? Extreme fatigue, daily steroids, and stress eating didn't help the situation. So as I sat on my couch recovering from surgery, I devised a plan, researched, and prepared to change my life. I had to; my daughter deserved the best possible version of me!

I am a goal oriented person so setting a goal was a good place to start. How about a 5k? Seemed lofty for someone stuck to a couch on doctor-prescribed rest time. *I can do it - no excuses*, I told myself. I needed to find a race but also give myself enough recovery time to succeed. Now, I love great fundraisers and I found a race linked to one of my passions: football at my alma mater, Penn State University. The race supported the Special Olympics and finished at the 50 yard line of Penn State's Beaver Stadium.

It seemed too good to be true. My surgery was in September and the race was in April. It could work.

Time for a training plan. Alright Google, I thought, let's get to work. I certainly had the time to research and that I did. I found a program for 5k novices by Hal Higdon. It was simple to understand and eight weeks long. I had plenty of time and needed to consider my recovery, so I rewrote it to go slower and take longer. I had a plan.

Before you run, you need to walk. Once I was given the green light to exercise it was time to focus on my plan and goal. It started with walking and thinking about my life. Surgery can put everything in perspective. How is your time being spent? What do you enjoy about your life? What do you need to change? What obstacles are in your way? How do you overcome them? This time spent alone walking, thinking, and planning was eye-opening. I needed to walk to clear my head and prepare for my journey. My pituitary wasn't likely to start working again, so I had to adapt to my new life and give it my best effort.

Eventually the walk became a jog. Some of the weight started to come off. My confidence grew. I had the realization that yes, I have a chronic illness but that illness doesn't define ME! This is my life and I am done making excuses. Yes, I will take all the pills every day, put on the medical creams, take my daily shot, but I am the one in control. One thing I quickly realized though is that I needed help on this journey because it wasn't going to be easy.

We all need help, plus it is more fun to work toward a goal with a friend. Now, my wife is FAST... like, college runner FAST. So that ruled her out as a running buddy, but she could participate in the race, too. Good plan, but on to the next idea. My brother-in-law, Big Al, and I are pretty similar individuals. We're both Penn State graduates and we did marry sisters, so we have that in common. I talked Big Al into joining the race with me and soon we added another college buddy. Ryan is a huge Penn State fan and alumnus, so it was pretty easy to talk him into it. Unfortunately, Ryan lives about four hours away so he was great for moral support but not a great running buddy. Still, I had a team.

I stuck to my plan, avoided obstacles, felt a little better every day, leaned on my friends, and then set my goal: run the whole 5k without stopping. Life was back in my control.

Race day finally arrived. I was emotional all morning. I stood at the starting line with Big Al, Ryan, and my wife, nervous but excited. I was ready. Somehow this event became way more significant than a race to me. If you had told me about that moment a year before at Myrtle Beach, I would have laughed in your face. The race began and my wife left with the leaders.

Big Al, Ryan, and I were quiet but focused. I thought about my doctors, nurses, my daughter, family, my wife, and all the work we put in to get to this point.

The finish line was within reach. There is something about crossing a finish line. All the work, all the pain, everything is for this moment. I entered the stadium with 50 yards to go. My wife and family were there to cheer me on. No thoughts, just running. The steps got a little faster, the breaths a little deeper. *Just you and your goal within reach. Take it,* I thought. Crossing that finish line was monumental in my life. It is hard to express what that race has meant to me. That moment gave me my life back, just like I hit reset. I planned, I worked, and I said NO to excuses.

We continue to run that race every year. Our team has grown, and I now run it with my daughter. Eventually the 5ks turned into 10ks, half marathons, and even a sprint triathlon. It all started with planning on the couch and eventually walking. I had to feel as if I had some control over my life again, and that is what the first 5k did for me. The thing with a chronic illness is that it's never going away. You can try to ignore it, you can pretend you don't have it, but it is there and part of your life. Accept it and never let it have control again.

Chapter 3

You Are Not Alone

One of the main reasons I wanted to write this book is to tell someone that he or she is not alone. Being chronically ill is one of the loneliest feelings you can have. Your loved ones can try to understand, but they don't. You feel so alone because NOBODY understands what you are going through. I have a wonderful support system, but at the end of the day they don't get it. Well, *I understand* that feeling.

It can be really hard when you have an illness but look completely normal. People label you as lazy or a complainer and it gets into your head. Eventually you may shut down, stop reaching out, or stop talking about your problems. I promise you it won't help anything if you ignore your issues. Trust me. I've tried, and only ended up feeling more alone.

I have spent so much time just trying to be normal, feel normal. I never truly accomplished anything until I accepted myself for what I am: an individual with a chronic illness which cannot be understood by healthy people. It's really not their fault, either. They try, but it's impossible. Truthfully, that is okay! I don't want anyone to pity me or suffer with me. I just want their love and support. I *need* it.

Trying to explain your illness can be an awful experience. It's confusing to others. All they see is a healthy looking person standing in front of them. *Could this person really be that sick and still look completely normal? It must be an excuse to be lazy.* New relationships can be a real struggle. When we're already coping with so much, the anxiety of attempting to build new friendships can feel overwhelming.

When you've told people about your condition, has anyone responded, "at least it's not _____." Obviously we are thankful it's not the worst case scenario, but don't minimize our struggles! This may sound stupid, but there was a time in my life that I wished I had an illness I could fight and have the opportunity to overcome it. Like, "I beat cancer" or "I am a survivor."

With a chronic illness there is no winning! Success for us is accepting your illness, but never letting it dominate your life. I understand your struggles. You are not alone. Don't be mad at your family or friends because they can't relate to your struggles. It isn't their fault! It can be so hard, so lonely, but you need to accept it and be okay with it.

As a young adult, I had a girlfriend who suffered from anxiety. I tried to support her and understand, but I couldn't. You try to be supportive, but in the back of your head you're thinking, *just knock it off so we can go to the concert,* or *another night stuck on the couch.* I was too immature for a serious relationship (and apparently growing a tumor that sent my hormone levels all over the place.) The truth is that I tried to understand, couldn't, and became frustrated. The karma is that I now understand what anxiety and depression are, and I wish I had done more to be patient and help her.

I have friends and family members who will read this book and I believe it will be eye-opening for them. I don't talk about my struggles. I am a stubborn guy who always does my best to hide the suffering. I don't want to be pitied. They don't understand anyway, so why complain? My super supportive wife has read some of my manuscript and stated that it opened her eyes! The person that helps me the most in this world doesn't understand, but loves and supports me anyway. That is all that matters!

You may feel alone, but you're not. Build your inner circle of friends and family for support. They don't need to comprehend what is happening in your head to show you love. Don't get angry or frustrated with people that don't understand. It won't help anything and it's not fair to them. Accept yourself and don't try and pretend you are a normal, healthy individual. Just be you, learn your limitations, and plan around them.

This is the hard part: you need to learn to love yourself as you are. The people you call friends already love you, so stop hating yourself because you have a chronic illness. It's not your fault! Cut yourself a break. Find things that make you happy. Let yourself be happy. Get the pity party out of your head. Stop thinking about your illness 24 hours a day, 7 days a week. I've been there and I am sure you have been, too. Your chronic illness isn't going anywhere and neither are you, so get off your couch, wipe away the tears, and learn to love your life! You only get one shot at this, so stop wasting time.

If you believe in turning negatives into positives, try this one: having a chronic illness can be a blessing because you appreciate the small things more. It's true. Take a moment to think back to how defeated you felt on some of your worst days. Maybe you're still struggling through them right now. Embrace the little moments and never take one second for granted, again. Hug a little longer, say thank you more, laugh, savor the good days, and just live in the moment.

Maybe you're not ready for positives yet and that's okay, too. It is hard to love yourself when you are struggling and battling every single day. How can you love yourself when you are questioning your existence? When you are wondering if your family is better off without you? I battle depression, but I am finally at a place in my life where I can say, "I LOVE MY LIFE." You can get there too. It will take work and you have to put in the effort, but eventually you can learn to accept your life and love yourself again.

I wasted years on excuses, depression, and getting in my own way because I hated the way I felt. I couldn't see a future with any success in it. Trust me, if I dug myself out of that hole, I have faith you can too. I hope I can help you avoid some of the time that I lost. You are not alone and you can succeed too.

Chapter 4

Desperate for Change

It is hard to accept your chronic illness as part of your life, and it is even harder to turn your new life into a success story when all you can see is the darkness. When I sat down and brainstormed how to describe someone successfully living with a chronic illness, the same words kept echoing in my head: *Perseverance*, *Grit*, and *Desperate for Change*. Let's take a minute to look at those words and phrases and see if they describe you.

Desperate:

One Merriam-Webster Dictionary definition of the word *Desperate* is: suffering extreme need.

Are you desperate for change? Look at that definition, SUFFERING EXTREME NEED. Not just trying to change, but wanting it so badly that you SUFFER extreme NEED.

Desperate is the attitude you need when you want to change your life. If you just try, you might fail. If you are DESPERATE for change, my money is on your success.

I want you to be DESPERATE in your approach to changing your life. I've been to the bottom and wondered how I could continue living when I couldn't even control the thoughts racing in my head. All I wanted was for the racing thoughts to stop; I wanted energy to live; I wanted just one good day. I wanted all of this, but was doing nothing to achieve it. I felt terrible and needed more, but put forth no effort for change. I was consumed by the darkness, symptoms, lack of energy... and gave in to all of it. It doesn't have to be that way! Even if you only improve a little each day you can write your own success story. It won't just happen, but if you are desperate for change, I believe you will achieve it.

When I wrote down my steps for change, they caught me off guard. They spelled the word DESPERATE. Crazy right? Okay, I did a little juggling of words but I still found it neat that one of the descriptive adjectives for success was an acronym for the blueprint of my plan. Take a look:

Dream

Evaluate your Situation

Study

Prepare/Prepare for Obstacles

Evaluate your Plan

Rank (Prioritize)

Ask Why?/Ask Why Not?

Team

Enjoy

We will walk through these steps together in the next chapters. I'll show you how I prepare and plan for goals in my life. You need a plan to succeed. You need to put in the work, but I promise you that your life can improve. If you're desperate, you can take your life back.

Please remember this is *my* blueprint for improvement. If something doesn't work for you, change it. This is just a blueprint. I looked back at my successes and failures and figured out what I did right and wrong. The first thing I do when I have a new goal is write it down. I will show you how I plan my process and give you some examples. Will it work for everyone and every problem in the world? Probably not. However, I can honestly say I have had success with a lot of adversity. My goal in writing this book is not to change the world, get rich, or get famous. I hope to help at least one person who is desperate for change. Maybe that person is another panhypopituitarism patient, maybe someone preparing for surgery, perhaps just someone ready to change their life. I hope my blueprint can help guide you through the change you desperately need in your life.

Grit:

Grit, as defined by the Merriam-Webster Dictionary, is firmness of mind or spirit; unyielding courage in the face of hardship or danger.

There have been days in my life where just getting out of bed seemed like an impossible goal. The racing mind, questioning my existence, always asking *why me? Why did this happen to me?* I had pain in my legs, and I'm not talking soreness… I mean PAIN. I'm sure I am not the only person with a chronic illness who has felt this way. You don't feel courageous at all. But eventually you take a step, then another one. You wipe away your tears, and maybe you go for a walk to hopefully clear your head. Now *that* is courage in the face of hardship. Look what you have overcome just by getting up. You are the definition of grit. Your family and friends won't see it, but I do, and you should too.

You demonstrate grit every single day of your life. To succeed with a chronic illness, you simply have to. You have to take that first step. You have to get out of your own head, dismiss the doubts, and believe in yourself. I'm not saying you should run a 5k tomorrow, but why not walk around the block? Next, look in the mirror and tell the person in front of you that you're proud of them and recognize the grit they showed today. Tomorrow, go a little further and believe in yourself. Think about your success as you walk. RECOGNIZE IT. You have so much courage. You are taking the first steps to change your life forever. You are not defined by your illness; you are more than your illness; you are courageous in the face of hardship.

Recognize your courage one step at a time, and keep going. This is not a sprint. Our successful journey spans a lifetime. We'll start compounding successful hours into days, into weeks, into months, into years, into decades, into the life you deserve. Your courage and grit will take you there.

Perseverance:

Perseverance is defined by the Merriam-Webster Dictionary as continued effort to do or achieve something despite difficulties, failure or opposition.

"Persevere" describes what an individual with chronic illness does every day. The difficulties are there and aren't going anywhere. Nobody's struggles are exactly the same, but we probably have some similarities. I've been living with my illness for 10 years. Some periods of that time were the lowest and worst of my life. I still have struggles and I always will, but now I have a plan in place for when they arise. My energy has greatly improved with my individualized exercise plan. Do I wish I had more energy? Certainly, I do, but I am proud of how hard I work and how much my energy has improved over the last decade. Do I still crash? Definitely. I've had days where I went to bed after dinner and woke up 16 hours later. I've accepted that as part of my plan, and I keep moving forward. We persevere. We must prepare for difficulties, accept failures, and keep battling to improve.

Let's look at that definition one more time. Perseverance is *continued effort to do or achieve something despite difficulties, failure or opposition.* Take a moment to think about opposition. When most people think about opposition, they think about an external force preventing your advancement. When I look back over the last 10 years, the opposition I see is an internal battle. The chronic illness we have is part of who we are. It isn't something we can avoid or forget. One of the hardest battles is accepting the illness as part of you and taking the first steps to improve and move forward. It is hard to get to that point because you feel AWFUL.

The first couple of months after my diagnosis were hell. I had never taken a prescription pill until that point. All of a sudden I was taking Levothyroxine, Prednisone (later switched to Hydrocortisone), Ativan, Zoloft, Androderm patches, and Cabergoline. I was constantly working with my endocrinologist to minimize side effects, switch medicines, evaluate progress, change another medication, combat worsening depression, change another medication... it was a really hard time. Maybe you're going through a similar struggle and it consumes your every thought. Your whole day is about how you feel and which medication is making you feel that way. What do you do next? Should you call the doctor? Every second of every day is about your illness. All you can do is try to persevere. You are showing massive amounts of courage, but nobody knows it and you can't see it.

Eventually, I realized that I have to take these medications to try to replace what I lost from my pituitary. What can I do to change my thought process, accept my illness, and move forward? What can I do for my anxiety, instead of constantly popping a pill that puts me to sleep? How can I battle the depression, besides taking these numbing medicines? What can I do to get more energy? How do I take my mind off of my illness and start living again? The medicines I take are a part of my life, but they alone are not the cure to all of my struggles. It was hard for me to see that when I was newly diagnosed. I was expecting the medicine to transform me back to my normal, old self. It is hard to accept that normal is not your goal anymore. Your goal has changed to constant improvement and a successful life that you love. We adapt, we show courage, we persevere.

I am no longer that 31 year old praying to return to normal. It took time, work, courage, and perseverance, but I was desperate to change and love my life again. I do, I really do LOVE MY LIFE. From time to time I look back at pictures of my 31 year old self just to see how far I have come. The struggles in my life have molded me into the person I am today. I wouldn't be who I am today without those struggles. That is all I want for you. I want you to see your courage, acknowledge your perseverance, and love your life. If you don't love your life, I want you to be desperate for change. Never be satisfied; keep improving. Work at it every single day and be proud of yourself.

In the next chapters I'll walk you through my process for change. I use the acronym DESPERATE to show how I devise a plan and chase my dreams. If you're desperate for change, maybe this process will work for you, too.

Chapter 5

Dream (Desperate)

The D in the DESPERATE acronym stands for Dream. Growing up, we all have so many dreams. We imagine and plan our perfect future. When you get sick, it becomes hard to think about tomorrow. All you can think about is how bad you feel at the moment. Your dreams turn into desperate prayers of returning to your former life and feeling healthy again. You need to try and dream again. Easier said than done, right?

You need to put positive thoughts back in your head. Imagine what you want for your future. Dream BIG. Don't think about the past when dreaming. We are going to move forward without staring into the rearview mirror. It is time to start dreaming again, and turning those dreams into goals, then into reality. Don't give up on your dreams; they may need adjusting, but never give up.

Some people have goals they've always dreamed about accomplishing. Some goals are found with self-reflection. Dreaming is important! It keeps you focused and keeps the goal on your mind. Goals help you turn your dreams into reality. Maybe the dream is something you wanted your whole life, like writing a book (not my dream), working at your ideal job, having six pack abs, running a half marathon, becoming financially stable, the list goes on and on. Or maybe it is a new goal, like setting a personal record on that half marathon, or getting a promotion at work. It just has to be very important to you.

I am going to walk you through one of my goals. My dream is to develop a healthy lifestyle, so I can keep my body as healthy as possible. One of my goals to accomplish this dream is to maintain a healthy weight. My weight has always been a struggle, but I am DESPERATE for change and ready to give it my best shot.

DESPERATE for Change- Maintain a Healthy Weight (Dream)

I already told you about my brief running career, but I injured my back (white water rafting) and had to do some adjusting. I've never really been able to lose weight by running. When I'm in a running routine, I am always, ALWAYS hungry. Well, I stepped on the scale right before my fortieth birthday and I was at 199 lbs! *Not again!* I was not going over 200 again. No way!

This time was going to be different, so I sat down and started working on a plan for myself. First, I evaluated my current situation: I was obese, very low energy, low self esteem, had failed on diets before, and was unsure if I could even lose weight. I have panhypopituitarism, which means I will be taking steroids for the rest of my life. Is it even possible to manage my weight while taking steroids? I decided to give it my very best effort and see what happens. I grabbed a notepad and a pen and wrote my goal in capital letters - MAINTAIN A HEALTHY WEIGHT.

If you haven't figured it out by now, let me inform you that I am a daydreamer. I love to let my mind wander and see what kind of ideas come to me. So, I started thinking about what a healthy diet meant to me. I didn't want a fad diet; I wanted something sustainable for my lifestyle. I also enjoy exercising, but I wanted a plan that didn't hurt my back. I needed something to give me some strength, and hopefully more energy. I hoped to see some results early on, so I could gain confidence and start believing in myself. I daydreamed about what being and feeling healthy would mean to my family and me. I decided I need this change in my life and it was time to get ready. Now, go write down your goal and let's start building our plan together.

My Dream: A Healthy Lifestyle

Goal: Maintain a Healthy Weight

Chapter 6

Evaluation (dEsperate)

The E in my DESPERATE acronym stands for Evaluation. Sometimes we are unable to see our goals or dreams. I've been so sick at points that a healthy lifestyle seemed laughable; I was just trying to make it through the day. Sometimes we need to take a look at ourselves and do some self-evaluation.

The goal with self-evaluation is to find your weakness and the obstacles in your life, so you can build a plan to avoid, eliminate, or minimize their effects. It can be hard to look in the mirror and be completely honest with yourself. *Maybe my weight gain isn't from steroids... could it be from the stress eating? Am I giving my best effort? Am I prioritizing unhealthy habits over exercise?* It is time to make a list of as many obstacles as you can think of, so you can make a detailed plan. Be prepared to stumble during your journey. What if you plan for how to handle the stumbles when they occur? You can't let the bumpy road put an end to your journey. You need to get up, dust yourself off, and refocus on your goal.

It is time to grab some paper and write down every excuse you've ever used, all the obstacles you face, and everything you can think of that might get in the way of your success. The following example is from my self-evaluation.

DESPERATE for Change - Maintain a Healthy Weight (Evaluate)

I've tried to lose weight before and I've failed. What did I do wrong? What obstacles will I have? How can I prevent failure this time? It is hard to evaluate yourself and find weaknesses, but if you don't know your obstacles how can you plan for them?

- ☐ I am always tired. Like I could take a nap right now, tired. I need to find a way to make exercise a priority.

- ☐ I need a diet that is sustainable. I've had success with counting calories, but that gets old. I've tried the Mediterranean Diet and enjoyed the food, but didn't have much success. I need to find a diet that I enjoy and I won't get sick of. I like carbs; I am not avoiding carbs.

- ☐ I need to keep my anxiety under control and avoid stress eating. I always reach for food when I am stressed.

☐ I need to incorporate some strength training into my daily exercise routine. With limited energy how am I going to accomplish this?

☐ I need to get my family on board with my goal. My wife is the main cook and I will need her full support to reach this goal.

☐ I've always struggled with restaurants and eating at friends' houses. How can I avoid this? How can I eat healthier at restaurants?

☐ I hate feeling hungry all the time. How can I minimize that?

☐ My back hurts. How can I avoid pain, improve my back strength, and keep exercising?

☐ Depression. How will I react? How can I keep on track when it hits?

Once you evaluate yourself and the obstacles in front of you, it is time to study and start planning. If you are not careful with your evaluation, you might get blindsided by an obstacle and give up. Evaluate, so you can be prepared.

Chapter 7

Study (deSperate)

We have a dream. We have a goal to help us reach that dream. We found our weaknesses and obstacles. Now it is time to study, so we can make a plan. A goal without a solid plan is simply a wish. We need to design our plan, but we need the knowledge to develop the perfect plan for us. I love to study. Whether it is reading about a topic, watching TEDtalks, podcasts, or getting opinions from individuals who I respect or look to for guidance. I love gathering information.

DESPERATE for Change - Maintain a Healthy Weight (Study)

For my weight loss goal, I went straight to Google and started searching. I knew I didn't want a low carb diet because for me that is not sustainable. I like carbs and cutting them out will lead to failure. I've counted calories in the past with success, but eating less of the same crappy food is not what I was looking for. I wanted to eat food that would benefit me - BUT good-tasting food. Vegetarian diets are not possible or realistic for me. Eventually, I came across the Mayo Clinic Diet. I already loved the Mayo Clinic Website (for information gathering, of course) but I had no clue they had a diet plan.

I decided to purchase the book and it was everything I was looking for - great recipes with a plan for success. Then I saw a cookbook, so I got that too. I'm not going to lie and say their plan is easy. It takes work, but I was DESPERATE for change.

Next, I needed to study a little more to come up with an exercise plan. Running was out, because it hurts my back too much. Cardiovascular exercise is very important to me because I truly believe it helps control my anxiety and depression. I have an old junky elliptical, so I gave it a try and it still worked! Now remember, I have limited energy and on some days I have NO energy. I tried exercising at different times of the day and found that I had the most energy and the least distractions in the morning.

I knew I also wanted to do some strength training, but I am too cheap to get a gym membership, don't have the energy to make this a priority, and I don't want to lift big weights. I just want some definition. I decided to try body weight exercises and found some apps to help keep me motivated. Then I found some YouTube videos to follow. I knew what I needed to do, but sometimes it's just nice to hit play and follow someone else's guidance. It helps keep me focused, especially early in the morning when I am still half asleep. I also have a chin-up bar in my house. I could NEVER do chin-ups (I believe my all time record might be 3), but it might be fun to try, anyway.

Having found my resources, I was ready to develop a plan for exercise and healthy eating. It was time to look at my weaknesses and obstacles, do a little more studying, and make a plan.

OBSTACLES/WEAKNESSES

I feel hungry all the time!

Luckily, my new diet plan prepared me for this. My goal was to eat at least 4 servings of fruits and vegetables each day. That is a lot of eating.

I've always struggled with restaurants and eating at friends' houses.

For this one I got advice from someone smarter than me: my wife. She said that we would eat out less, look at the menu before going out to eat, and take healthy food along to our friends' houses. We could eat unhealthy foods in moderation and fill up on veggies or fruit trays. She is clearly the brains of this operation.

I need to get my family on board with my goal.

Done, nothing to study. Turns out that they want a healthy father/husband as much as I want to be healthy.

I am always tired. Some days I have zero energy.

This one I had to study myself. I already know I have the most energy in the morning. Now when I say that, I want you to know I am NOT a morning person. The hardest part of my day is the first step. I SNOOZE, then SNOOZE again. My wife eventually kicks me out of bed and I start my day. The energy appears, but not the second I open my eyes! I am so jealous of morning people, but I am desperate for change, so morning exercise is best for me. I know that on some days I will have zero energy. Those days will come no matter what. I needed to accept that and prepare for it as part of my plan.

I need to keep my anxiety under control

I have been studying this for years! I hate anxiety attacks! I've identified some triggers and I try to avoid them. One trigger for me is large crowds. It is challenging because it is a common denominator, but doesn't occur every time.

One of my favorite hobbies is watching my Penn State Nittany Lions play football or hockey. I love sports. Beaver Stadium holds

107,000 amazing fans. I love the energy of live sports. Television can't capture that for me, so I want to be there.

Sadly, one of my worst anxiety attacks happened during a football game. I felt terrible: near tears, nauseated, sweating, restless, and sensing that something was terribly wrong, but I had no clue what it was. My wife immediately saw it in my eyes. It was a great game, but the anxiety consumed my every thought, ruining the experience. Unfortunately, I didn't have any Ativan with me and I just couldn't take it anymore. The tears started flowing. I told my parents that I needed to go. My dad was shocked; I NEVER leave games early! My wife grabbed my hand and led me out as I tried to hide my face. This has happened at a few games, but I refuse to give up something I love.

Another example of a trigger for me is a place called Funland at Rehoboth Beach in Delaware. Every year we visit my best friend at his family's beach house, on the bay in Delaware. I love the trip but DREAD going to Funland. My daughter LOVES Funland. Only my wife knows of my pure hatred for that place. The crowds, the noise, the spinning rides making me nauseous, the heat, the smells.... Wow do I hate Funland, but I love my daughter more than anything. So, each year we go and it takes two seconds for my anxiety to begin. I can't watch her on the rides without feeling like I am going to throw up. I usually take two trips to the disgusting bathroom just in case, and to avoid the experience for a few minutes. I walk out to the boardwalk for air, but the crowds are everywhere. I always take Ativan for this occasion, but the anxiety is too much. I hate every second of it, but I will continue to do it for my sweet, little girl.

We can't avoid every situation that brings anxiety, so you either have to deal with it, or plan for it. Don't stop living. My best treatment for anxiety is staying active, taking my Ativan when needed, and attempting to eat healthy.

Depression, how will I react?

Depression is awful. I am not an expert on depression, and I won't pretend to understand what you are going through, but I will try to explain my battles. I would guess that 90% of the people I know have no clue about my struggles with depression. If they do know about it, they have no clue how bad it actually is. I'm a stubborn guy. Stubborn guys hide things, we are macho, and we keep secrets because that's what men do. Depression can come out of nowhere and turn your life upside down. I wish I had all the answers, but I don't. I am a work in progress; I take one day at a time.

I've read a lot of books on depression. I wish I had a favorite to recommend for you, but most of them are written by people who studied depression. That is fine and I always come away with some good tips and strategies, but unless you experience that feeling you will never truly understand it.

Everyone's struggles with depression are different. I am not looking for sympathy. Truthfully, I don't even want to talk about depression, but if I can help one person it's worth it to me. I've been the guy who couldn't find the strength to get out of bed, the guy who slept for 16 hours straight, the guy with head to toe pain, and the guy crying uncontrollably in his car, wondering if he can do this any longer. This is not easy to type or even think about, but I will tell you about two episodes of my severe depression. I'll do my best to remember what it felt like in the moment.

Years ago I worked for a couple (I'll call them "Mr. & Mrs.") who were very influential in my life. Mr. is one of my heroes because he was my mentor on how to be a great husband. Mrs. was funny, kind, ornery, and her eyes always lit up when she had an opportunity to pick on me. Unfortunately, Mrs. also suffered from dementia and had cancer. Mr. never left her side; he was amazing. They were truly meant for each other.

When Mrs. passed away, it was probably the hardest "non-family" death I ever dealt with. The funeral was packed and beautiful. Just seeing the pain in Mr.'s eyes was hard for anyone to handle. All of his days were built around his wife, every second, and now he just looked lost. His pain and sorrow were killing me.

I am a fixer and I couldn't fix him. The individual who taught me how to be a better husband couldn't hold in his emotions anymore.

I left the funeral an emotional DISASTER and it just started to free fall from there. At home, I pulled into the garage and just sobbed uncontrollably. I physically hurt everywhere, couldn't breath, couldn't control any of my emotions, and couldn't stand. After a few minutes, my wife noticed my car in the garage. She hugged me and squeezed as tight as she could. I still couldn't stand up. I told her I needed help. I *begged* for help, and I am normally not someone who even *asks* for help. I couldn't calm down. She sat with me, listened, and waited.

Eventually, she got me to my feet and guided me to bed. She called my best friend (luckily also a Nurse Practitioner) and put him on speaker phone. I begged for help and we talked about going to the Emergency Room. I couldn't get up and I didn't want people to think I was crazy. Later, I found out that my wife and best friend made sure there was nothing in the bedroom I could hurt myself with. My body hurt so badly, my head was begging for relief, and trying to breathe was exhausting. Eventually, I depleted all my energy and fell asleep.

Exhausted, I slept in bed or on the couch most of the next few days. I had no motivation to do anything, extreme fatigue, exhaustion, and pain everywhere. It took a long time to recover from that episode, but I did learn a few things. First, I need time to recover. The pain is real, the exhaustion is extreme. My body was put through unbearable stress. The fatigue was real and I needed to recover. *Let yourself recover.* Second, I needed a push to get moving again. My wife was patient, but she got me up and made me go for a walk. She made me talk about what I was going through. She supported me wherever I was at that day, but didn't take no for an answer. I might have stayed in bed twice as long, but she got me to take the first steps to recovery. Finally and most importantly, I learned that there would be sunshine again. I had been to my bottom, questioned my existence and picked myself back up. I could breathe again. I could find good things in my life. I had survived. It was an awful ride, but I came back and learned ways to improve. I persevered.

In the next example, nothing specific triggered my depressive episode and recovery took much longer. It was a normal Pennsylvania winter snow storm. My wife and I shoveled the driveway, then played in the snow with our daughter. Winter time can be hard: so dark, cold, and isolating. That night, I had some pain in my legs and felt tired... but I'm always tired. The next day was awful. My legs and arms hurt badly. I was EXHAUSTED. With no motivation to do anything, I just wanted to sleep. I slept all day. The next day was the same, but I didn't care. I didn't want to get up. I hated the way I felt but was too sad to care about anything or anyone. I pushed my family away in favor of sleep. I hated myself. I thought, *why do I feel this way? I'm not worth the time and effort my wife puts in to deal with me. I'm not worth anything and they would be better off without me.*

My head was awful, the pain was real, and I had zero intention of ever getting out of bed. I was in a very dark place. Maybe you've been there. The anger, the sadness, and the pain can't be explained. I don't expect to understand your feelings, but I want you to know you are not alone. I eventually recovered from this dark place with my wife's help. She never gives up on me. I took one step, then two… eventually my legs stopped hurting, eventually I smiled, eventually I started living again.

I hope and pray that episodes like these will never happen again, but I learn more about myself each time they occur. With a routine exercise program, I've had fewer episodes. I've learned that staying active and trying to stay positive can help decrease their frequency. I know now that if I feel depressed I need to get up and go for a walk. I need to move. If I continue to lie down, I'm not going to get better. I've learned to work with my doctor for optimal medication management.

I hate depression and anxiety, so I work hard at prevention. I've tried acupuncture, yoga, meditation, chamomile tea, a chiropractor, and more. I constantly look for ways to improve because I need to keep going. This is my life and I don't want to spend it in bed wondering why I am even here. Keep researching, keep trying, and find what works for you.

I need to keep the negative out of my head.

I'm going to slip up. I am going to have a bad day and binge eat. I'm going to have wings one day. I need to control my thoughts, accept that it was just one bad meal, regroup, and keep going. Sometimes our minds can make mistakes seem bigger than they are and convince us to quit. I can't quit, I NEED to do this. Stay positive with your thoughts. Be proud of your effort. Mistakes will happen - be okay with it. Just don't let the mistakes continually repeat or you will fail. Learn from your mistakes and have a plan for when they happen.

That is what we are going to talk about next. It is time to develop our plan for change. We did the work; now, let's put it together and see what we came up with.

Chapter 8

Plan (desPerate)

It is time for the most important part of the process. We have a clear goal, we know our weaknesses, we've identified obstacles, and now we're ready to use that information to design a plan for success. We are developing a plan that will work in your life and help you make the change you are desperate for. Please remember to be realistic with your plan. Don't plan to run two hours per day, seven days a week if you are a new runner. That is not sustainable or realistic. Be honest with yourself. Let's get started.

DESPERATE for Change - Maintain a Healthy Weight (Plan)

During my studies, I was very excited when I found the Mayo Clinic Diet. The diet was everything I was looking for. I wanted to eat healthy, but also enjoy the recipes. My wife and I picked out a few of our favorite recipes and wrote a menu for the first week of the diet. We set a start date and prepared a grocery list.

We also planned to try new recipes with fruits and vegetables to see which ones we enjoyed the most.

I bought a calendar with lined spaces to write on individual days. I decided to record my weight and exercise program on the calendar and my daily food intake and servings on the individual days. All of the preparation made us feel excited and very motivated.

I wrote out my exercise program. My cardio goal was 30 minutes on the elliptical machine most days of the week. I set my alarm for 5:15 AM hoping to be on the elliptical from 5:30 AM to 6:00 AM. Since I'm most energetic in the morning, this schedule would prioritize my energy and limit distractions. Next, I scheduled my strength training using body weight exercises and light weights. I had about 20 minutes between the elliptical and when I had to get ready for work. I had already found some YouTube videos with great 10 minute ab workouts, so I scheduled them every other day. On the days between ab routines I planned to do back extensions to hopefully help my sore back. I found an app on my phone for a push-up challenge. I just needed to hit start and follow along, which is good because I don't like to think in the early morning. I decided to alternate push-ups one day, chin-ups and weights the next, then a rest day, and repeat. I also added a stretching routine. If I was running ahead of schedule there was even time for deep breathing meditation.

I know I will always have some days with no energy. Instead of scheduling my off days, I take it day by day. Working full time, I usually run out of energy by Wednesday or Thursday. One of these could be my off day, and maybe Sunday if necessary. I never want two days off in a row. It just doesn't work for me. I don't want to lose focus or mess up my routine.

My wife made our plan concerning restaurants and eating at friends' houses. We planned to eat out less overall, and to look at the menu online before leaving home when we go to a restaurant. When we'll be eating at a friend's house, we can take a healthy tray along to guarantee we'll have at least one healthy option. We also decided we needed occasional cheat meals. Restaurant visits or going to a friend's house would be a good time to schedule a cheat. We could prepare earlier in the day, by having fewer servings or extending our workout for the day.

I thought it would be harder to get my family on board, but they were ready and excited to start. Okay, my daughter (nine years old and a picky eater) wasn't excited, but she was willing to give it a try. Not that she had a choice, anyway.

The last part of the plan was my biggest concern: how to reduce my depression and anxiety. My plan was to get as much early success as possible and keep building on that. I truly believe that exercise helps my anxiety and depression. I decided that even if I have a bad day I should take a walk for exercise. My support team was ready to help me with any difficulties I came across. I was also worried about stress eating and how hungry I feel when I am anxious. We had already rid the cabinets of junk food, so my plan was to reach for carrots or celery. I wasn't sure if that would work, but it was worth a try.

The plan was laid out: stay active, deal with stumbles quickly, and avoid stress eating. I knew adjustments would be needed throughout, but I felt prepared to face my obstacles. There would definitely be hurdles. If this was easy, I would have done it 8 years earlier! Now it was time to evaluate my own readiness and rank my priorities.

Chapter 9

Evaluate and Rank (despERate)

We have a plan and a separate plan for dealing with obstacles. We are almost ready for change. The next steps in the blueprint are Evaluate and Rank (or prioritize.) Yes, we are going to evaluate again! This time we are evaluating our goals with the knowledge we gained from studying, and with the plan that was designed for OUR needs. Are you ready for your goal? Are you DESPERATE for change? If the answer is yes, then set a start date and prepare. Just make sure that your priorities are right.

As an example of this step, one of my longtime goals was to be a volleyball coach. Both of my parents coached and I was lucky enough to receive a scholarship to play in college. I love the sport and really believe I could be a great coach. Well, when I sat down and re-evaluated my life with that goal, I decided it was not the right time. Coaching takes a lot of time and dedication. My energy is not limitless; I must constantly prioritize my energy and health over other goals. Would I love to coach? Well, yes. Is it more important than family time, my exercise routine, and my health? Nope. I don't need the extra anxiety. The team would deserve my best and I am not sure I can offer anywhere near that right now. Maybe someday.

DESPERATE for Change - Maintain a Healthy Weight (despERate)

Back to my weight goal. I selected the diet plan and designed a workout plan. I set a date and wrote it on the refrigerator calendar. My wife was on board with the plan and my daughter was not very excited, but agreeable. We wrote a menu, made a shopping list, and copied recipes we wanted to try.

We decided this lifestyle change was an important priority in our life. We set aside exercise time (all three of us in the morning) and a cooking prep day (Sunday) to get a great start on the week. It was a team effort and we were ready.

Maybe your goal is self-improvement or health. When you take the time to prioritize, I want you to give yourself permission to be a little selfish. Sometimes, if you are DESPERATE for change you need to prioritize yourself! With my exercise/weight loss goal I was getting up at 5:15 AM! Remember that I have limited energy, so that means in bed by 9 or 9:30 PM at the latest. I saved my hardest workouts for the weekend. Scheduling can be hard. Social interactions are essential, but you may need to adjust them to fit your goal.

If you are trying to lose weight, going to restaurants is hard and stressful. So why not fire up the grill and have your friends come to your house, instead? If you decide to go to the restaurant, take the stress out of ordering by looking at their website and menu first. Decide what to order before you leave the house. Enjoy the social time with your friends. You can always adjust your workout, if needed. Enjoy the process of achieving your goal, but don't sabotage your goal. Remember, one bad night or mistake will not ruin your goal, but your reaction to the stumble could. Relax, refocus, and go get your dreams.

Chapter 10

Ask Why? Ask Why Not? (desperAte)

Why do you want this goal? My daughter's first year of life was difficult. I was very sick. I went part-time at work due to sickness and the need for child care. That was the hardest year of my life.

My why is: I want to be my best every day for my wife and daughter. Could an illness come from nowhere and disrupt my plans? Sure, but it won't happen because of my actions or lack thereof. I want a healthy lifestyle. I work every single day on my mental health. My family is the most important thing in the world to me. They are my WHY.

What is your why? Is it self-improvement? Maybe to improve the world? Maybe to improve your current situation? The reason can be anything, but the answer is so important! You are going to have hard days; there will be struggles on your journey. This will not be easy. If it was easy, you would have done it by now. This time will be different. As you write out your dream and your plan, I want you to write your WHY in capital letters. On those hard days, look at that piece of paper and remember why you are so committed this time. It's why you are SUFFERING extreme need for change. Usually the reason for change is bigger and more important than any of the struggles.

Ask yourself, *why not? Why not me? Why can't I do this?* Then STOP MAKING EXCUSES. Wow, do we make excuses! I do it, too! I tell myself that I can't lose weight because I take chronic steroids. I think I can't run a half marathon because it is too much of a time commitment. I feel like I can't exercise because I am too busy. I can't... I can't... I can't... Get out of your own way!

Why not you? *Well, because I have a chronic illness.* Yes, these are the cards we have been dealt and it isn't fair, but we need to stop making excuses. *My energy level is low.* Well when is it good, focus your scheduled goal to that time and prioritize it. *My depression is too bad.* Yup, been there. Get studying, try every coping mechanism, and work with your doctor to improve your life. This is your life; this is your story. Get your excuses out of the way.

YES, we have obstacles and I am 100% sure you will have challenges along the way. Plan for them and don't let anyone or anything get in the way of YOUR success. You are not defined by your struggles. If anything, they made you grittier and more determined. Go look in the mirror and tell yourself, *no more excuses! This is my life and I deserve better! Nothing is going to stop me!*

Chapter 11

Team (desperaTe)

You always need a strong team behind you for support, motivation, cheerleading, assistance, or maybe even to work on goals with you. Having a strong team also makes changing more attainable. First, you need to find your inner circle of support. The ones who get you through the toughest times, but also the people you would do anything for and they know that.

I am so lucky to have a strong team. As I think about them, I realize that I'm attracted to friends who are driven to succeed and family-oriented, but also fun, positive people. Here is my Dream Team:

The Glue - My wife is Superwoman. Life would feel impossible without her love and unwavering support. She is strong when needed, always supporting and motivating, and picks me up when I am down. She truly is the glue that holds everything together in my family and my life. You need someone that believes in you, even when you may not. It could be a spouse, a friend, maybe even a co-worker. Remember, that this is not a one way street. You need to spend time and energy supporting them, too. Sometimes we can take our support system for granted. As anyone with a chronic illness knows, we can be exhausting! My wife does so much. Appreciate your support system, thank them, and always make sure they know how much they mean to you.

Friend you can lean on - When I am down and can't pick myself up, my wife always does her best to fix me. Sometimes it is too bad to get up. That's when I know my phone will start to ring and keep ringing until I finally answer. It will be my buddy Brent calling.

Brent and I met about 17 years ago at my first job out of graduate school. When I graduated, I wanted to work at the nation's #1 heart hospital, doing stress tests. I got the job and moved to Ohio, where Brent joined the team a few months later. We were instant friends and drinking buddies. Beer pong, Nintendo video games, grilling, and hanging out with Brent and his wife, was pretty much my normal routine. Eventually, I met Superwoman and moved back to Pennsylvania, but my friendship and bond with Brent were cemented. Our families are very close considering we live in different states. His kids are basically another niece and nephew, and my daughter loves them all. We vacation together yearly and visit when we can.

Brent is a hard-working, driven individual who understands what's happening in my head when I can't even figure it out. We are basically brothers from other mothers. Brent has the ability to help me get out of the darkest places depression can take me. He listens, understands, advises, and eventually gets me to laugh. He helps my wife pick me up when the depression is too heavy for just myself and Superwoman. A heavy burden is more manageable with more people holding it.

Brent is always there to support my wife as well. For this I am eternally grateful. Even Superwoman needs a little help sometimes. Thank you Brent, we love you, and you'll never know what your friendship means to me and my family. Everybody needs a friend to lean on. Don't forget to tell your friends how much they mean to you, and never take their friendship for granted.

My Daughter - Magical Hugs. Love you.

Family - I am blessed with a supportive family. If I am struggling, my parents show up and take care of our daughter, to give me the time I need to pick myself up. They have always been there for me, and I know they will always be there when needed. I also have a wonderful sister, in-laws, brothers-in-law and sisters-in-law, nieces, nephews, cousins, aunts, uncles, grandparents… I am truly blessed with family support.

Social Friends - You also need friends that can help take your mind off everything. Friends that make you laugh and distract you from hardships. That's Dave, Joy, and the girls. Dave is a driven, goal-oriented family man. Are you finding a pattern?

Dave has no filter and Joy is the boss of the family. It's a fun combination to be around. Nothing matters more to them than their two daughters, great girls that I am thankful my daughter calls friends. One of our favorite things to do is just relax around a campfire, either at Dave and Joy's house, or on a camping trip. Sometimes I just need to relax, have some wine, and enjoy life. Friends like them just make life easier.

My inner circle is a big part of who I am. Any of these people would do anything for me and they have proven it time and time again. Always work on your inner circle. Find support, plant friendships, and see what grows from them. You never know when life will come in and change everything, so have your support system in place and ready. Talk to these people about your dreams/goals and let them enjoy the ride with you. Cheer them on and support them as they chase their goals. *Always* prioritize these relationships.

Another important part of your team is your doctors. My endocrinologist and primary care physician are definitely on my team. Find doctors who listen to you and your opinions. I research; it's what I do. I make suggestions to my doctor. Why are people scared to do that? It is my life! My PCP is young and listens well! I love discussing ideas or things I researched. I want to learn from smart people. At one appointment I asked about trying a new medication because I'd read an article on its positive effects with the atypical depression sometimes seen in panhypopituitarism patients. Atypical depression, as defined by the Mayo Clinic, means that your depressed mood can brighten in response to positive events. Symptoms include weight gain, sleeping too much but still feeling tired, heavy or leaden feelings in arms or legs that last an hour or more in a day, sensitivity to rejection or criticism... Yeah that sounds like me. My doctor did some research and we decided to give it a try. It's working and life is getting better. It's not perfect, but better. Thanks, Doc.

Doctors should work with you. They should care about your opinion, listen, and be able to educate you about your condition. This is your life, your body, your mind, so make sure you are part of the process. Provide feedback and ideas. Find doctors that you can work with because they are an essential part of your team.

One last avenue of support that I want to mention is social media. I am not into social media as much as the average Joe, but I still glance at it occasionally. I do use support groups on Facebook. These are other, similar people going through whatever it is you are battling. Facebook groups can be a great place to meet, even if they're scattered around the world. Support group members might understand you and your struggles. *Disclaimer - Find the right group for you. If a group is not what you are looking for, keep looking.*

Two groups I am a member of are the *Hypopituitary Support Group* and *Panhypopituitarism*. I don't contribute much, to be honest, but when I read about everyone's struggles I realize I'm not alone. Maybe that is why I am writing this book. I struggle, but I have learned to embrace and love my life. Sometimes, I read people's posts and think back to when I was saying all the same things. I want to yell at my past self: *It's time for change, this is your life. Embrace it, turn the negatives into positives, improve every single day, and chase your dreams. Get out of your own way. Yes, you have problems but battle them! Don't give up! Dream, then achieve.*

Here is one of my posts from five years ago (11/1/2015):

"Thank you for letting me join the group. I have been feeling very alone and nobody understands. My quick summary started 5 years ago when a pituitary tumor was discovered and I had surgery to have it removed. Unfortunately, it was too late for my pituitary to be saved.

When I first got my diagnosis I did everything I could to fight it. Started running, made a goal list (½ marathon, mini-triathlon, 72-mile hike), and accomplished them all.

But I'm sick of the routine (pills, patches, shots) and I've come to the realization that this is a battle that I can't win. I'm not going to get better and I'm constantly wondering what the effects of all these pills are? I never had anxiety or depression, but now I'm in a constant battle. I have support but nobody really understands. Does anyone else feel this way?"

I got 21 comments that day, and the support was overwhelming.

You are not in this alone. If you need someone to motivate you, you can message me. I would love to hear your story, your dream, your plan. I want to be a part of your team. Maybe we can support others with a DESPERATE for Change group. I'm in. You are not alone, build your team one person at a time.

Chapter 12

Enjoy (desperatE)

This is the easiest step: ENJOY! Enjoy the entire process. Enjoy your accomplishments! Celebrate small victories. Be proud of yourself. Take a mental picture of what it will look like and feel like when you cross that finish line. That is everyone's favorite part of the race - that feeling when you have reached your goal. Enjoy the emotions, remember the struggles, think about all the obstacles and adversities that you overcame. Celebrate!

My weight goal has been reached. Yeah, I have a chronic illness. Yeah, I take daily steroids. Yeah, there were obstacles, but I was DESPERATE for change and I knew my why. As I am writing this, I weigh 158 lbs. My goal was to maintain a weight between 155 and 160 lbs. I have way more energy! I feel healthier. My mind is so much calmer, less anxious. My depression is under control for now. I like the person I see in the mirror. I enjoy eating healthy food. I can do 100 push-ups in a row and actually have a little muscle definition. I can do 18 chin-ups (my all time record before this was three.) Was it hard? Yes! Was it worth it? Hell yeah.

There is something special about reaching a goal when you have a chronic illness. That illness will always be a part of your life, but you feel like you took back control. This is my life and I am in the driver's seat. Sometimes that is hard to see, which is why you need to enjoy the whole process. It's about taking back control of YOUR life. Overcoming obstacles, making a plan, and guiding yourself to success. A goal without a plan is simply a wish. Enjoy the entire process, be proud of yourself, and take back control.

Keep Dreaming/Adjust goals:

You DID it! Enjoy it! Just don't ruin it. You worked too hard and have come too far. Take time to celebrate, but keep going. If you had a health goal, now it turns into a maintenance goal. If it was to run a 5k, now what? A 10k? A faster time? Celebrate your accomplishment, but keep going. Adjust. Look in the mirror at that gritty, accomplished person, and find a new goal. Don't relax, you are taking control of your life. Keep going.

Chapter 13

God's Plan

Each and every one of us is writing a story. We have a beginning, a middle, and an ending. What we do in the middle is up to us. It is a blank sheet of paper.

My story consists of chapters of health, sickness, and the new me. The hardest part was figuring out the new me. Life pushed the reset button on everything I thought I knew about myself. The honest truth is that I had some tough years in the middle chapters. When you are ill, it consumes you. You overthink everything. *My head hurts, why does my head hurt? Do my meds need to be adjusted? Is the tumor back? Why am I so tired? Is my thyroid level off? Do I need more testosterone? Did I take my HGH shot last night?* It doesn't stop and creates a lot of anxiety.

Dealing with a chronic illness is hard, and you need to work with your doctor for optimal treatment. But the hardest thing is to accept your illness for what it is. It is a part of your life, but don't let it consume your whole life. I did that too, all the time. *I'm sweating, why am I sweating?* It doesn't stop; we are scarred.

It is time to accept your reality, but remember that your illness or adversities don't define you. Once you accept yourself as you are, then it is time to improve. The rest of your story is just blank sheets of paper awaiting fresh ink, with the ending still to be written. We don't know when the story ends, but we control the narrative. Too many pages of my story were used for worrying and not living. Questioning, not working. Blaming, not enjoying. We must turn the negative to positive and start living. This is my story, and I will control it.

All those years of *why me? Why did this happen to me?* It is weird to have a chronic illness but look completely healthy. Nobody understands! *Just why me?!?!* STOP IT! Please stop wasting your life. Learn from my experience and don't waste your precious time. Accept the struggles and start living.

My tumor was removed nine years ago. Now pay attention to what I am about to say: I LOVE MY LIFE. I never thought that would be possible again, but I truly love my life. It's definitely not perfect and it takes a lot of work, but what a ride it has been. I can honestly say I have more great days than awful days now, but I am in the moment for all of them.

I'm to the point of my journey that I can look back at cherished experiences that only happened because I got sick. This may sound stupid, but having a chronic illness has made me a better person and more grateful for everything I have. Crazy, right? Trust me, if I could change some things I would. If my pituitary started working tomorrow, it would be amazing. But after nine years I know it won't come back and I've accepted that.

Think about everything you have. Think about everything you've accomplished since being sick. Even the small wins are huge, so be proud of them. Let yourself be proud. You are gritty and I want you to write an amazing story.

I often question if this was God's plan for me all along. Maybe I was on the wrong path. My illness made me slow down, enjoy the little things, and even resulted in a career change. I was sick long before I realized it. Sometimes I wonder if I would still be at the #1 heart hospital if I hadn't started to get sick. Would I have met Superwoman? I messed up several relationships before that, so why did it work once I got sick? Where would I be now? Maybe it all worked out like it was supposed to. Accepting that is hard, but eye-opening.

When I started my professional career I was ambitious enough to know I wanted to work for the #1 heart hospital in the country. Well, that's not what I do today. I used to put heart transplant candidates on a treadmill and push them to their limits. Talk about high stress, but I loved it. I couldn't even imagine doing that today. I would be popping Ativan all day. It's hard to believe that was my job.

Now, I am an Activities Coordinator working with senior citizens. Sometimes, when I am calling BINGO or leading a balloon volleyball game I wonder, *how did I get here?* I needed a job with less stress and it turns out I love working with seniors. This still feels weird, like I'm wasting my talents. However, I made the decision to make my life, health, and family the priorities over my career. I wonder if that was part of God's plan, too. I've been lucky to meet some truly amazing people in my job. Let me tell you about a few:

"Gussy" was an amazing 94 year-old woman. We called her Gussy because when she got excited she said, "Oh Dear Gussy!" Gussy and I were instant friends and her eyes always lit up when she saw me. Gussy made my day, too. She was always ready to make me smile and share a laugh. We always joked that I was her favorite staff member and an adopted grandson. My friend Gussy passed away last month and I will never forget her. At her viewing, several of her family members approached me and said, "You must be John. She was always talking about you." Her granddaughter had found a picture of us together and included it on Gussy's memorial board above the words "Adopted Grandson." Gussy's memory will forever be in my heart. Maybe she's one of the reasons I am where I am today.

Another individual I will never, ever forget is a WWII veteran who I'll call the "War Hero." He was one of the nicest individuals I ever had the pleasure of meeting. Plus, the War Hero loved his baseball. We developed a close relationship and I loved visiting and just socializing. Unfortunately, my good friend fell and when I visited him in the hospital, he wasn't doing very well. I was the last person to have a real conversation with him. When he passed, I was devastated by the loss. I tried to hold it together. Then I saw his son and had a conversation with him in which he asked me to be a pallbearer at my hero's funeral. I accepted the humbling invitation. When he left, I locked myself in a locker room bathroom and wept uncontrollably.

My heart hurt so bad. I wondered how I could continue to do this job and keep getting hurt so badly. Then I realized how important these connections were to me. I had made an impact on his life and clearly he touched mine. Isn't that what life is all about? I promised myself that the day it stopped hurting, was the day I needed to find a new job.

Another friend, the Mayor, as everyone called him, seemed to be known by everyone. He was a man who spent his entire life as a proud farmer. Well, he was pretty ornery and so am I, so we had an instant friendship. Once, the mayor stole my microphone, took it to another room, and started broadcasting, "John, John, what are you doing?" He couldn't stop laughing over that one. My wonderful co-workers assisted my friend's family in helping him have a peaceful passing at home. I miss my friend every day, but I am thankful for the memories and laughs that we shared.

Sometimes I wonder how I ever got here. It has been one crazy roller coaster ride with so many highs and lows. Without the tumor, I don't think I would have switched careers. I really don't. I never would have met Gussy, the War Hero, or the Mayor. I never would have felt that extreme pain when I lost them. I know it's just a job, but I've given it so much of my time and passion, that it became more. These individuals and so many more have changed my life forever. The heartache just proves that I gave them my heart. My heart will recover, but the memories they left me will last a lifetime. I'm not sure if this was God's Plan all along, but I am thankful for and blessed by all of these experiences.

Chapter 14

What Now?

After I reach a goal, adjust a goal, or go into the maintenance phase, I take a little time to evaluate where I am and where I want to be. I believe in taking a holistic approach to wellness. You can google all the dimensions of wellness and decide which ones mean the most to you. I focus on Physical, Mental, Spiritual, Social, Occupational, and Financial wellness. I have goals for each group and if I'm not happy with my progress, I start developing a plan for change. Wellness is more to me than just my physical health.

Self-improvement means more than being skinny or running a 5k. It could be finding a career that makes you happy, finding supportive friends, building a relationship with God, or maybe finding financial stability. I use a calendar to track my exercise and diet. At the back of the calendar there are blank pages for notes. I dedicate a page to each dimension of wellness that I listed above. Each page has a definition of what that dimension means to me and strategies for me to achieve that goal.

When I review my list, I constantly look for ways to improve. For instance, when COVID-19 came along and I found myself trapped at home by my beautiful and concerned wife, I had time to re-evaluate my progress. And yes, I really do mean trapped in my house. She once didn't let me out of the house for 8 days. That's when I realized I am not the only one who bears scars from my surgery.

With the time I had, I reviewed our financial situation. One of our long term family goals is to be debt-free and retire to a small cabin with some land near the Penn State campus. Well, somewhere along the way we lost focus. I did some nerdy math and realized we were giving way too much of our hard earned money to the bank to pay for our debt. We had been living life in cruise control and forgot about our goals. It happens, unfortunately.

We walked our goal through the DESPERATE acronym, and now we are back on track. We paid off one vehicle and we are now focused on paying off my car, so we can start attacking the mortgage. We also took advantage of some record low interest rates to refinance and shave 15 years off of our loan term. We made our goal a priority again and we are desperate to change our financial future.

This goal is really important to me. I love my family. I want to protect them always. Once you've been sick, you don't feel as invincible as you used to. I often think about all the medications I take and wonder what side effects they will have on my body in the future. I won't be around forever, and I want to know that my family is protected if something happens to me. That is my why. I need to make this goal a reality, so I can sleep better at night, knowing my family is taken care of.

This goal is going to take some time (10 years or less) and lots of discipline, but we will get our little cabin in the woods. Someday, I'll sit on my screened in porch enjoying a cup of coffee, as I beat my wife in a game of cards. The dream is crystal clear, the *why* is very important to me, and we will remain focused to change our financial future.

That is why it is essential to write down your priorities, review them often, and look for weaknesses or areas for improvement. I can't focus on more than one or two goals at a time because honestly, I don't have the energy. I need to rank my priorities and decide what is most important to my family and me. If you try to do too much at one time, you will lose focus and the odds of you failing will keep increasing. Find areas for improvement, make a plan, and stay focused.

Chapter 15

The New You

This book was written by an individual with a chronic illness. I am not a doctor, psychologist, scientist, or even a published author (at this moment). I struggle. I have my bad days. I don't have all the answers. I set out to write a book that tells my story, so maybe someone out there won't feel so alone. If this book reaches even one person suffering and gives them encouragement, then it was worth every second.

I offered a blueprint outlining how I've had some success in change. You are welcome to use my ideas, but you can design it to fit your lifestyle. I promise I won't be mad; I will applaud your efforts.

Adversities don't have to be illnesses. They can come in many shapes and forms; and everyone has them. Accept them as part of your life, make a plan, then write YOUR story. Own your successes and failures; just promise me you won't stop dreaming and trying. My story unfortunately has chapters of nothing but sadness and doubt. Listen closely; It doesn't have to be that way. Take back your life, take control. It is your story.

Never stop dreaming. Never get complacent. Keep improving. Re-evaluate after reaching a goal and start again. Keep moving forward. You are gritty. Be desperate for change.

Occasionally, life will come along and hit the reset button. Take it as an opportunity to re-prioritize your life. Evaluate, but don't let adversities write your story. Turn the negatives into positives. Maybe changing careers is the correct path... who knows? Perhaps another change is coming. I don't know, but I will enjoy the ride.

YOU ARE MORE THAN YOUR ILLNESS! That sounds like common sense, but I've lived through periods of life where my health consumed my every thought. It was impossible to have a real life that way. Your illness doesn't define you. Yes, it is part of your story but look at what you overcome every single day. What a *success story*!

Lastly and most importantly, I leave you with this thought: love your life or become desperate for change. I want you to love your life. Accept your obstacles, but don't let them be excuses. Dream. Build your inner circle. Study. Be or do whatever you want. Be proud of yourself. Stop asking, *why me?* Ask, *why not me? Why can't I accomplish that goal?* You can! You always could because you are a dreamer, you are gritty, and you are desperate for change. Love your life, keep improving, write a beautiful story, and be desperate for change.

Acknowledgements

I never expected the *thank yous* to be the hardest part of the book to write, but they certainly are. How can I thank everyone who has been there for me, supported me, prayed for me, and touched my life? I can't. It is not possible to express in words what these friendships mean to me. If I wrote about every person who has left a fingerprint on my heart, this short book would become a novel. From the bottom of my heart, THANK YOU, I love you, and your friendship and support is everything to me.

I do need to recognize a few individuals because without them I would never have been able to write this book.

My Ladies - Laura and Sydney. You always support me, pick me up when I am down, and love me unconditionally. You even support my crazy ideas like writing a book! You are my world and my happiness revolves around the two of you. Thank you, love ya.

My Parents - Thank you for everything. You've never stopped supporting me or believing in me. It's been a rollercoaster ride, but your unwavering love and friendship has been by my side during the whole journey. You both have always believed in me, even when I didn't. I could never thank you enough for everything you have done for me and my family. Love you both.

To my massive family and friends. My sis, brothers-in-law, sisters-in-law, parents-in-law, cousins, aunts, uncles, grandparents, Godparents, roommates, tailgating buddies, co-workers, the list goes on and on…. Thank you for being part of my story. I couldn't recognize all of you individually, but each one of you have impacted my life, and I am eternally thankful.

To my doctors and nurses. Thank you for always being there for me. I literally wouldn't be here if it wasn't for you!

To Andi Whitaker. The first person (besides my wife) that I let read my manuscript. If you hadn't believed in me, this book never would have happened. I trusted your opinion and your honesty; you didn't let me down. You took my terrible English and awful spelling and turned it into something I am truly proud of. Thank you for supporting me and making this book a reality.

To Dave Freidenbloom and Nancy Kennedy (my other editors/support team/friends). Thank you for your time and efforts on my manuscript. You believed in me and pushed me to finish this project. Thank you.

Last, but certainly not least, THANK YOU to everyone who took the time to read this book. I hope my story motivates someone to want more from their life, believe in themself, and then desperately go after their dreams. Someday, I hope to hear your story of grit and perseverance as you desperately pursue a life worth loving.

Printed in Great Britain
by Amazon

60503026R00058